Coffee

the
BEAN of
MY
EXISTENCE

by R. D. Thomas

an addict

AN OWL BOOK

HENRY HOLT AND COMPANY ● New York

Henry Holt and Company, Inc.
publishers since 1866
115 West 18th Street
New York, New York 10011

Henry Holt ® is a registered Trademark
of Henry Holt and Company, Inc.

Published in Canada by Fitzhenry & Whiteside Ltd.,
195 Allstate Parkway, Markham, Ontario L3R 4T8.

Library of Congress Catalog Card Number: 94-78612

ISBN 0-8050-3769-1 (an Owl Book: pbk.)

Henry Holt books are available for special
promotions and premiums. For details contact:
Director, Special Markets.

First Edition — 1995
Printed in the United States of America
All first editions are printed on acid-free paper. ∞

1 3 5 7 9 10 8 6 4 2

this

BOOK

is

dedicated

to

hopeless

addicts everywhere

but especially TO↑ Beasty,

audrey and Emma . . . .

THE WORST OF THE WORST

(with *love*)

Take this SIMPLE Test.

WHAT DO

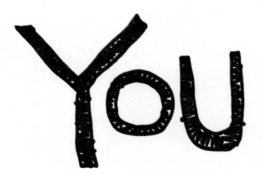

Think THESE Are?

delicate

no nonsense

chic

diner

pure gold trim

botanical, yet modern

arty

reigned for less than a year

CORONATION OF EDWARD VII · 1937 · KING · HO · HN

hint *

ATHENA

16 °½

cardboard

very very big

if YOU said CUPs...

GUESS AGAIN

those fragile Vessels

ARE THE TOOLS

of an ADDICT

I Kid YOU Not

FACT:

IN YOUR TOWN. In MY TOWN. MaYBe in YOUR NEIGHBOR'S House. maYBe in YOUR OWN HOUSE!!!

THERE ARE OVER

100 MILLION

USERS IN America

HiDDEN BeHiND CLOSED DOORS!

The ADDICT may use FILTERS MUCH LIKE those below.

FILTER

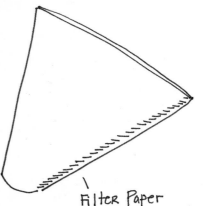

Filter Paper

But the absence of these IMPLEMENTS does NOT

I KNOW.

COFFEE is my

MUD
JAVA
BROWN GOLD
JOE

THE
BEAN

THE ELECTRIFYING JOLT OF CAFFEINE

HERE IS MY TRUE FACTUAL STORY.

It's really all

MOTHER'S
FAULT

(isn't everything?)

FEEL FREE!
DRINK COFFEE!
DRINK WINE!
HAVE A SMOKE!
ENJOY!

note: in those days, Doctors didn't warn expectant mothers **NOT TO DO ANYTHING FUN** during pregnancy

There She SAt.
Naïvely sip sip SIPPing coffee for
40 weeks. morning. Noon.
And NIGHt. WAITING for
Me to BE BORN. MY POOR
addicted MOTHER didN't
KNOW what she WAS
DOING!

FIGURATIVELY SPEAKING

THE
BEAN

had taken hold of
her LONG AGO

AND AS YOU SEE, THIS IS A VERY BIG BUT

to hear MOTHER tell it. Things could have been WORSE. I was a **WONDER** baby.

WALKING.

TO DRINK OR NOT TO DRINK **TALKING** STION. TO DRINK PERCHANCE FEE IS THE QUES COFFEE CCCCC COFFEE

translating the **Bible** from **GREEK.** AND THEN INTO JAPANESE!

mom's

doing calculus.

...and doing it fast.

MONTHS

before the

OTHER

BABIES GOO GOO GOO GOO

MOTHER

SIP sip SIP

SIPPETY SIPPED

and I SAW oh yes, there was NO mistaking IT

I SAW

What IT did to

her OTHERWISE BORING and VIRTUALLY MEANINGLESS DAY IN DAY OUT DRUDGE OF A NUMBINGLY ROUTINE ROUTINE PICK UP SOCKS IRON DUST MOP SHOP COOK TAKE THE LINT OUT OF THE DRYER PAY THE BILLS CUT ONIONS UNTIL SHE CRIED AND CRIED ROUTINE ROUTINE Life

AND YET (bless her heart)
SHE ♥ NEVER COMPLAINED
(the saint) WELL. ALMOST NEVER
WELL. NOT ALL THE TIME.

one day MOTHER
Poured a few drops
of FRESH BREWED
COFFEE
into
my pristine
milk.

innocence perdu

From that moment 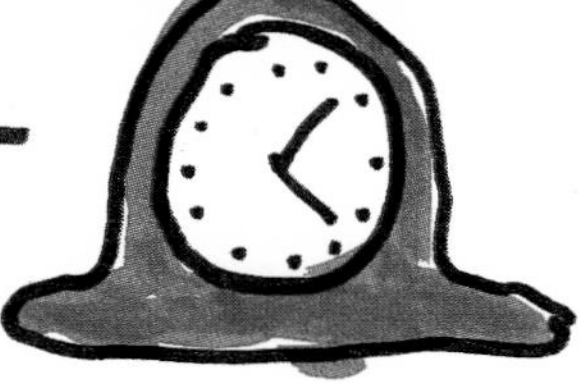

I was 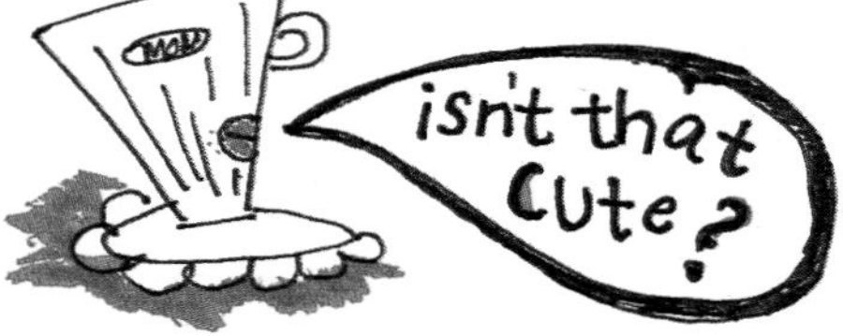

HOPELESSLY HOOKED

before you could say

JUAN

ValdEz

I was heedlessly yes! Recklessly Yes! a Thousand times yes!

DRINKING 1

 TWO

 3 EVEN

in PUBLIC PLACES

more! more! more! more!

EVERY

SINGLE

DAY

SUNDAYS!

LEGAL HOLIDAYS!

WITHOUT EXCEPTION

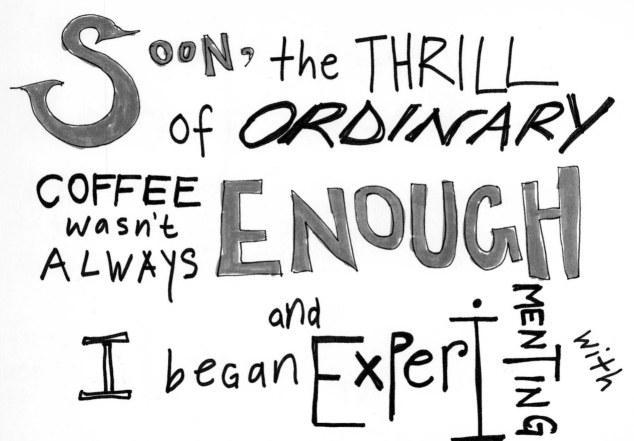

Soon, the THRILL of ORDINARY COFFEE wasn't ALWAYS ENOUGH and I began ExperImenting with

have you noticed how very **SEXUAL** the shape of the coffee bean is.?

EXOTICA

AND I WOULD GO TO ANY LENGTHS TO GET IT, BELIEVE YOU ME!

FROTHY topped CAPPUCINO flecked with chocolate

tiny cups of devastating TURKISH sludge

chic espresso from Italy

BLACK BEANS from the plains of KENYA

Jamaican blue

Bubbling Café LAIT au

mais oui

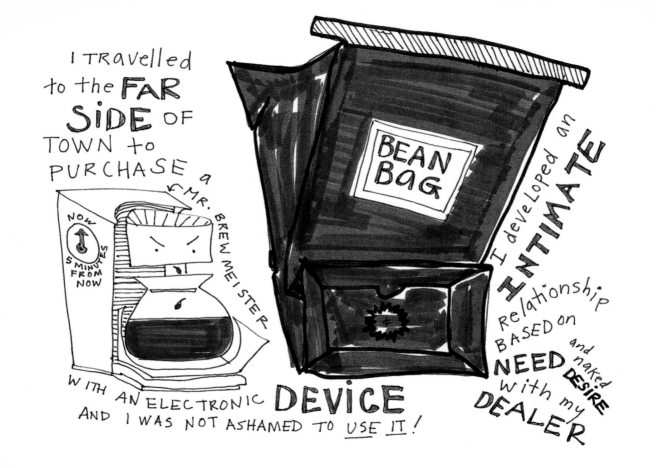

Not content to drink alone . . . .

I SHAMELESSLY
sucked treasured friends
and LOVEDONES

into the MADCAP CRAZY,
hedonistic SUPER CHARGED

SPIRAL

into . the
WORLD OF

COFFEE

are you SURE you
don't want just a
teensy weensy itty bitty inky dinky little
tasteepoo TASTE tasteywastey...
IT'S MY OWN
SPECIAL
BLEND

HAVE
another?

Was NO

CUP of COFFEE

"I'll express!" "we get you there!"

EXCEPT POSSibly in UTAH where THEY'RE MORMON and they DON'T BELIEVE in COFFEE. So if you order a cup GOD HELP YOU! They are going to make VERY SURE

ONE WAY ticket

YOU NEVER COMMIT THAT SIN AGAIN!!

I met someone I could

that special

Love

someone whose special special
company I could SAVOR

~~MORE THAN~~ ALMOST as Much as

that FIRST

FLAVORFUL MORNING

BREW

We were oh so **HAPPY!**

You're so sweet!

No, You're so sweet!

No!

We're both so... sigh....

You're wonderful!

No, you're wonderful!

No! We're both.... sigh...

IF YOU'VE EVER BEEN IN  YOU KNOW WHAT I MEAN.....

TOGETHER WE MADE **BIG PLANS**

WE WERE GOING TO WIN THE $20,000,000,000 LOTTERY AND LIVE IN AN 18 ROOM HOUSE WITH 12 WONDERFUL WELL MANNERED KIDS WHO NEVER INTERFERED WITH OUR ENDLESSLY **PASSIONATE** SEX LIFE ♥ AND NEVER FORGET the LITTLE Things thAT _REALLY_ COUNT ♥

THEN *isn't it ALways the Way?*

my DEARLY beL♥VED

Took me hOMe

To MEET the

FaMiLY

How was I to KNOW?

HOW WAS
I
to KNOW
iT WAS

THAT'S RIGHT.

DECAF

It could never be the same

after that.

I drifted for a while.

Roaming from Coffee Shop to Coffee Shop

drinking from the Bitter Cup

of EXPERIENCE*

* But at least it was

caffeinated experience

SHUDDER

CRUELLY offering MY
PERSONAL guests
A sMaLLeR cup than I SERVED
MYSELF

mine

yours
So
That I COULD HAVE
MORE MORE more
AND I STILL WAS NOT SATISFIED

WHY?
YOU MAY
ask..... LOOK AT it THiS Way. ON a GOOD WEEK

I was HAVING SEX oh Maybe

LET'S SaY SOMETHING LiKE, WELL, WHO's
COUNTING? MaYBe OH I don't KNOW . . . .

TWICE

AND I was HAVING

HOT HOT
HOT COFFeE

SURE thing AT LEAST just exactly
30 TIMES A WEEK the way I
like it

I awakened one morning after THE MOST EXTRAORDINARY BINGE

never To be FORGOTTEN

I had it ALL!

I did it all!

and then I did it again!

ONLY to find MY LIFE IN

COMPLETE AND UTTER RUIN

The waiter grinned THAT'S RIGHT.

HE GRINNED. WHO GRINS AT SOMEONE WHO HAS NOT HAD HIS FIRST STEAMING CUP of

LIFE GIVING COFFEE? I ask YOU

I SHOULD HAVE SUSPECTED HIM THEN and THERE. BUT I WAS too BLEARY EYED to GIVE HIS UNNATURALLY WHITE teeth AND HIS STAINLESS APRON a SECOND GLANCE.

MAY I HELP YOU? HE said.

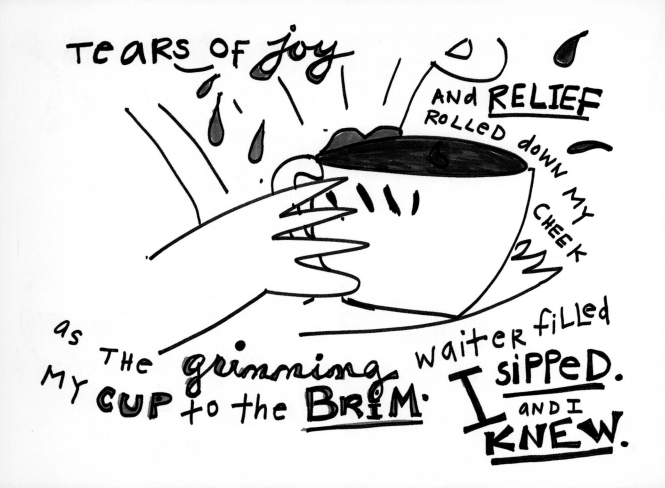

INSTANTLY That I had BEEN BETRAYED

And shouted

"" NOBODY

BUT NOBODY AND I MEAN **NOBODY**

PULLS THE MOUNTAIN GROWN

HOW THE HE—— DO YOU GROW @RYSTALS ON A MOUNTAIN?

FILCHERs ★

★ NAME CHANGED SO THEY DON'T SUE THE PANTS OFF ME!

INSTANT @RYSTALS SWITCH ON

ME! "

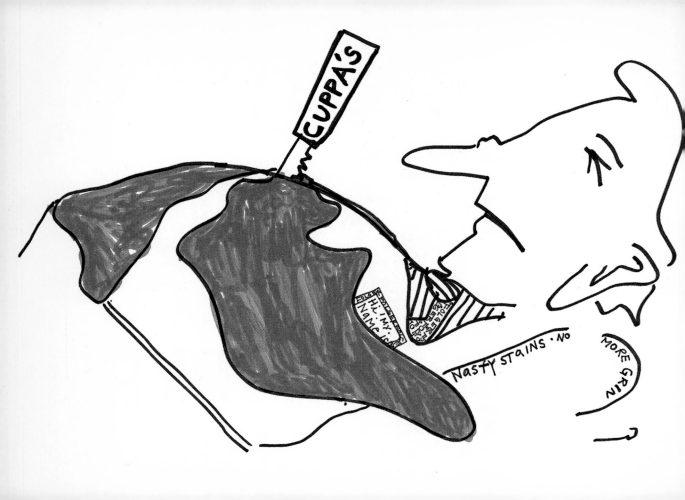

THERE WERE SEVEN / 7 / RELIABLE eYe WITNESSES

AND

A BROAD CAST QUALiTY ViDEO TAPE

OF THE CRIME

HEINOUS
HEENEEUS
HEYNUSS

A
C
CUPPAS
B
mount F___ cristo

NOT to MENTION ALL THE EVIDENCE RIGHT ON THE SPOT

JUSTICE
CE
was SWIFT

ANd HaRSH.

The Judge,

An unrepentant ten cup a day
man from way back,

Understood the **PAIN** and

SUFFERING

I had been forced to endure as a
result of this **VILE** act

AND as his **HONOR** personally poured **Me** and himself a good cup of fresh hot stimulating **JOE** — at last!

HE ordered those **LOW** down Crystal packing **PERPETRATORS** to get right back up their **ALLEGED** mountain **AND STAY THERE...**

but **NOT** before they atoned to the tune of **$1,257,340,000,000** payable to their sorry **VICTIM**, me.

UNBRIDLED Total Addiction COFFEE HAD NOT ONLY ENSLAVED ME

It had given me the BURDEN of Dazzling Amazing Extraordinary WEALTH

has bean

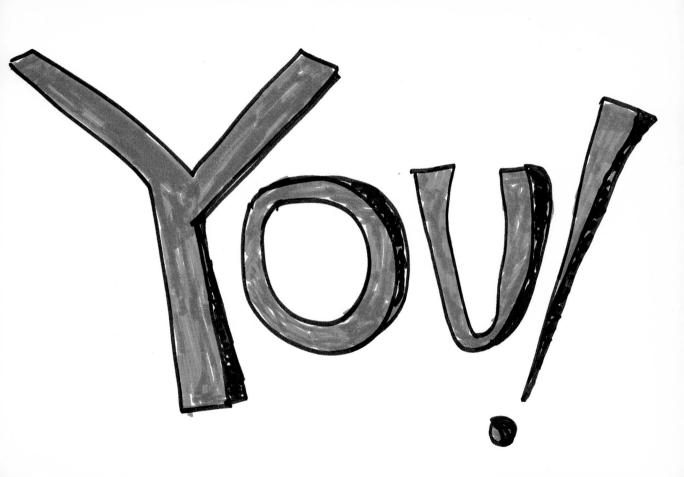

your name here

NOT the end.

TELLTALE SIGNS OF ADDICTION. ① COFFEE MOUTH (UNMISTAKABLE)

② TRACES OF FINE **BROWN** POWDER UNDER NAILS, ON KITCHEN COUNTERS, etc.

③ IRRITABILITY BEFORE 10 A.M. AND AGAIN BETWEEN 3:30 P.M. AND 5

④ NO VERBAL SKILLS BEFORE FIRST CUP

⑤ TENDENCY to PURCHASE AUTOMOBILES ON BASIS OF COFFEE HOLDER OPTION

⑥ MAY BE SEEN CLUTCHING EMPTY MUG AND CARESSING FULL ONE

THE ADDICTS CREED

COFFEE IS the air that I breathe the sun the stars the moon the staff of life the brown blood in my pulsating veins the VERY bean of MY existence and I will NEVER NEVER NEVER have ENOUGH I will NEVER EVER GIVE IT UP no way no how

⑦ TENDENCY TO FIND NEW FRIENDS WHEN OLD FRIENDS SUGGEST OR URGE THAT ADDICT CUT BACK ON COFFEE CONSUMPTION ⑧ BROWN CIRCLES ON FURNITURE AND OTHERWISE UNMARRED TABLE CLOTHS